CHIT-CHAT FOR ALL OCCASIONS

POLITICS

KNOCK KNOCK®
VENICE, CALIFORNIA

Created and published by Knock Knock
Distributed by Who's There, Inc.
Venice, CA 90291
knockknockstuff.com

ISBN: 978-160106112-6
UPC: 825703-50131-5

10 9 8 7 6 5 4 3 2 1

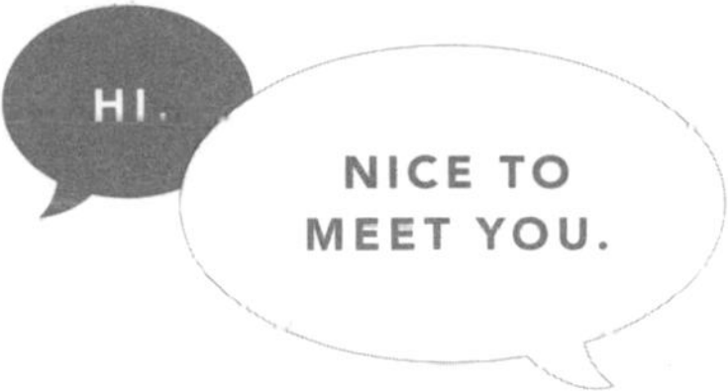
HI.
NICE TO MEET YOU.

TABLE OF

....
CONTENTS

HOW TO USE

One of the great pleasures of chit-chat is its brevity. This book is organized accordingly, broken into digestible bits and pieces perfect for sparking interest, offering interjections, or closing out a conversation. In addition to engaging facts and thought-provoking quotes, each chapter provides a number of useful guidelines for dealing with all manner of social encounter, represented by the following icons:

Know your audience, and use these helpful tips and tricks to navigate even the most
challenging run-ins.

REDIRECTORS

With these topical elements, you'll effort-lessly shift any conversation back to the matter at hand: politics.

Be successful in any social situation—and make all the right moves—with these savvy conversation suggestions.

INTRODUCTION
Getting the party started

....

Chit-chat is all around us. Whether you're at a dinner party, a family gathering, or mingling with coworkers after hours, there are few events in life that don't involve chewing some quantity of fat. Even before we leave the crib, we're preparing for a life of chatter. What is baby talk, after all, if not our first noble attempts at striking up a conversation? As we grow, however, we gradually refine our communication skills and, perhaps more importantly, our chosen topics.

Politics, for better or worse, is as inescapable as idle conversation. Ever since humans began to organize themselves into discrete groups (even ages before the fifth century BCE, the Athenians dreamed up the first form of democracy), politics has been center stage in our lives—and it's no wonder why. What other institution is capable of connecting us to global events even as it impacts our daily lives? As the twentieth-century congressman Thomas P. "Tip" O'Neil opined, "All politics is local." Considering the unique power of politics to ignite passions and spur debate even as it demolishes social barriers and unites compatriots, what better discussion topic could there be?

But the subject of politics also presents a challenge to aspiring chit-chatters. Like riding a horse, it's best to know what you're doing before climbing on. Forget left or right, liberal or conservative—the point is not to be elected. Rather, the goal should be to engage others in short yet memorable conversation. Given politics' ability to elicit strong opinions in even the mildest of tempers, some study of how to execute a successful discussion on politics is not ill advised.

The Chit-Chat for All Occasions series of books was made with exactly this study in mind, combining practical tips on conversing with an arsenal of ready-to-use facts, quotes, and other chatty tools. Useful both as a handy at-home resource and portable reference, this pocket-sized primer is guaranteed to prepare you for and deliver you from any number of social situations. In *Chit-Chat: Politics*, you'll learn how to initiate or defuse a wide range of political discussions, as well as how to redirect any conversation back toward politics. And because politics is nothing if not individual, you'll also find subject-specific information on potential audience members. For those new to chit-chat, you can simply use the information as it appears. For those more confident in their abilities, don't hesitate to add personal spins to a fact or rephrase an anecdote to create a unique effect.

And while most political careers tend to be longer than a standard conversation (a notable exception being Australian rugby star Mal Meninga, who reversed his decision to run for office mere seconds after announcing it), it's worth noting that there are many similarities between the two. After all, what politician worth his campaign button doesn't recognize the importance of engaging would-be supporters? Whether it's initiating dialogue, bolstering one's position, maintaining the status quo, or bowing out gracefully, each section in this volume will help you conduct chit-chat on par with the most clever spin doctor.

Finally, it should be said that politics is not always associated with the best of human endeavors. President Ronald Reagan, in fact, famously quipped that while politics was supposedly the second oldest profession, it bore a striking resemblance to the first. Don't let this deter you in your quest for political rapport. For every inclination to change the subject or avoid heated debate, there is an equally strong yearning to jaw about a nose-to-nose presidential race or decry the moral lapses of self-righteous government officials. In so many ways, politics is about life, and life is always interesting. So go ahead and throw your hat in the ring—running for office might require a small fortune, but talk is, well, cheap.

Primaries

Every politician knows that if you want to win an election, you have to join the race (write-in candidates aside, of course). Lucky for you, striking up a conversation is easier—and cheaper—than running for office. But practiced politicos do have some wisdom to impart on putting your best foot forward.

In a recent study by the International Society of Political Psychology, test subjects were shown photographs of congressional candidates. They were able to predict the winners based solely on their impressions of who appeared the least threatening. The lesson: first impressions aren't simply important in initiating successful conversations, they're crucial.

Of course, high-profile candidates benefit from an entire staff of handlers to primp them and prepare them for public engagements. You have only your good sense and this book—and that should be enough.

This chapter will provide everything you need to get the conversation started. You'll learn how to make an effortless entrance and how to perform the perfect political handshake. In addition to the invaluable tips, you'll be able to draw on the wise words of others (such as Harry S. Truman's classic quote, "Always be sincere, even if you don't mean it") and pepper your conversation with pertinent political jargon. Finally, with a bevy of facts, stats, and anecdotes at your fingertips, you'll initiate and navigate exchanges with total ease.

Being adequately prepared has the added benefit of bolstering your self-confidence, and nothing is more alluring than a confident chit-chatter. If you feel up to it, lend a signature touch to your conversation by adding flourishes to the information found in the following pages. Then, after successfully making your first pitch, sit back and open your ears. Your partner will revel in the attention, and you'll have plenty of time to plan your follow-up.

You're now ready to get the party started. Just remember that, like political masterminds, scintillating conversationalists are made, not born, so don't be dismayed by a few initial missteps. After all, every candidate has to start somewhere.

Upon entering the chamber of the House of Representatives to give the State of the Union address, the president traditionally doesn't rush when moving toward the dais. When making your own entrance, follow this presidential example. You probably won't have the benefit of a sergeant at arms announcing your arrival (or a rousing standing ovation of the nation's lawmakers to usher you in), but lingering near the door affords everyone an excellent opportunity to notice you. Remember, you don't have to win over a joint session of Congress, so just keep your chin up, smile, and move into the room. As you do, project confidence, warmth, and approachability, and shake hands, especially with those you're meeting for the first time.

An election is coming. Universal peace is declared, and the foxes have a sincere interest in prolonging the lives of the poultry.
—*GEORGE ELIOT*

waf•fle *vi* : to equivocate or dodge, usu. to avoid commitment or in an effort to mislead — *syn* FLIP-FLOP, VACILLATE, WAVER — *see also* POLITICS AS USUAL — "I love my wife, but I really **waffled** on my wedding day"

Waffling may be the norm in politics, but it makes conversation frustrating. Cogent thoughts are the backbone of chit-chat.

MUSIC

In early 2000, candidate George W. Bush agreed to stop playing Tom Petty's hit "I Won't Back Down" during campaign rallies after he received a cease and desist letter from Petty's publisher. To further his point, Petty performed the song for Vice President Al Gore on the event of his concession to Bush from the vice-presidential residence in Washington. Clearly, the tune resonates with contenders for office; other prominent politicians who have featured it in their campaigns include Virginia Senator Jim Webb, New Jersey Senator Robert Menendez, ex–New York Governor Eliot Spitzer, former North Carolina Senator John Edwards, Secretary of State Hillary Clinton, and Texas Congressman Ron Paul.

Which is more important in a candidate, intelligence or charisma?

Intelligence

How would you characterize the intelligence level of most politicians?

Bunch of idiots *Bunch of geniuses*

Should candidates be required to take an IQ test?

Yes *No*

Which politicians do you think would fail?

What subjects should it cover?

Is the average citizen smart enough to be a politician?

Doubtless *Doubtful*

What other job would prepare a person for office?

Do you expect big politicians to have big egos?

As a rule *With exceptions*

Does an inflated ego lead to political corruption?

Is there a place in politics for emotions?

Is it more important that a candidate know the issues or look good while giving a speech? Your fellow chit-chatter's response will help you steer the conversation.

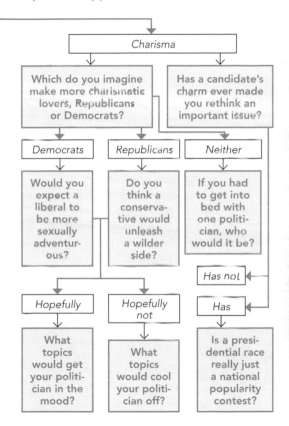

Charisma

Which do you imagine make more charismatic lovers, Republicans or Democrats?

Has a candidate's charm ever made you rethink an important issue?

Democrats

Would you expect a liberal to be more sexually adventurous?

Republicans

Do you think a conservative would unleash a wilder side?

Neither

If you had to get into bed with one politician, who would it be?

Has not

Has

Hopefully

What topics would get your politician in the mood?

Hopefully not

What topics would cool your politician off?

Is a presidential race really just a national popularity contest?

> *Hell, I never vote for anybody. I always vote against. —W. C. FIELDS*

Reference this quote to ask others if they've ever voted against as opposed to for a candidate.

....

WHAT'S IN A NAME?

Hopeful politicians looking for a leg up should check their birth certificates along with their credentials. While there has never been a tally of all politicians' names, past presidents have disproportionately been named James, John, or William. In fact, these names account for nearly a third of all presidential monikers. As for last names, five have been repeated, each of them twice: Adams, Johnson, Harrison, Roosevelt, and Bush. But while male politicians generally favor using their last name, the trend among female politicians has been to campaign using their first name instead, e.g., Hillary and Sarah. Pundits posit that the more familiar nomenclature will make the female candidate appear more approachable.

Not just a topic to bemoan, weather can be a political make-or-break factor. A 2005 study showed that bad weather on Election Day could increase the odds of a Republican victory. Undecided voters, who are historically more likely to pull the lever for a Democrat, are less likely to venture out if the weather is inclement. According to some experts, the dry spell of 1960 could even have influenced the Kennedy-Nixon election, giving JFK a leg up.

ANIMAL HOUSE

While almost everyone can recognize the donkey and the elephant as iconic party mascots, few are as familiar with those of the Libertarian Party (unofficially, the penguin) or the Modern Whig Party (the owl).

Everybody has a chance to become President of the United States. I'll sell mine for a quarter. —LAWRENCE LEE

TALK THE TALK

To lend an air of political authenticity to your conversation, try introducing a little *Pentagonese* into your lexicon. The unofficial language of the five-sided institution, this jargon is one way officials can obfuscate the truth, as well as increase their own sense of self-importance. For example, instead of "knowing what's going on," you can promote "situational awareness." For fear of coming off as pompous (or just plain creepy), though, use this technique sparingly.

FAMILY TREES

According to the New England Historic Genealogical Society, Hillary Clinton is a distant cousin of Angelina Jolie (a ninth cousin, twice removed, to be exact), Madonna, Celine Dion, Jack Kerouac, and Camilla Parker Bowles.

Asking new acquaintances casual questions about their families is a great way to establish conversational closeness.

> *To elect, and to reject, is the prerogative of a free people.* —*THOMAS PAINE*

With 36 percent of Americans claiming to
be Democrats, it's likely that you'll run into a
few now and then. While blue-state voters are
traditionally seen as liberal on many issues—
including health care, social welfare, and the
environment—don't assume that Democrats
take an identical stand on every issue. Feel
them out with a few telltale topics like immigra-
tion, gay marriage, and the federal deficit. Once
you get a sense for any particular leanings, try
using one of the items below either to spark
interest or initiate a healthy debate.

FOR:	AGAINST:
Public radio	Fox News
Big Government	Big Business
Living on a coast	Midwestern malls
Bob Dylan	Billy Ray Cyrus
Volvos	SUVs
Alternative fuels	Coal
Peace rallies	War
The New Deal	Reaganomics
Apple products	Guns
Yoga	Line dancing

....

FULL TRANSPARENCY

Before turning to politics, Massachusetts Republican Scott Brown was making head-lines—with his tan lines. In 1982, Brown was selected as "America's Sexiest Man" by *Cosmopolitan*, which featured a nude spread of the politico. While it's unproved whether Brown was the first aspiring politician to let it all hang out in a national rag, it's likely no one is going to challenge his title.

For the right crowd, talking about which politicians everyone finds sexy can make for lively conversation.

> **PETS**

Cats and dogs are fine for the masses, but over the years, politics as usual has meant some unusual presidential pets. Andrew Jackson had a parrot named Pol that he taught to swear, William Taft made room on the White House lawn for Pauline Wayne, a Holstein cow (and replacement of the less celebrated Mooley Wooly, a Jersey cow), and Benjamin Harrison kept two stately opossums named Mr. Reciprocity and Mr. Protection.

PARTY TIME

Yes, there are more than two. In fact, alternative parties have been making their voices heard in the brave new world since its beginning.

- **1792:** Democratic Party: *ye oldest party in the United States*

- **1854:** Republican Party: *the big tent on the right*

- **1869:** Prohibition Party: *taking the party out of party*

- **1901:** Socialist Party: *because Sweden really is sweet*

- **1912:** Communist Party: *classless doesn't mean no class*

- **1966:** Black Panther Party: *power (and lots of guns) to the people*

- **1971:** Libertarian Party: *civil liberties for all*

- **1996:** Labor Party: *working for change*

- **2001:** Green Party: *putting the Earth first*

- **2002:** Marijuana Party: *seeking high voter turnout*

I always voted at my party's call,
And I never thought for myself at all.
—*W. S. GILBERT*

THE RELATIVES

Like Maria Shriver, a Democrat, and her Republican husband, Arnold Schwarzenegger, sometimes family members don't see eye to eye on politics. It's probably best to stay away from the topic altogether, but occasionally it's unavoidable. If you're faced with a relative on a political rant (especially one that you don't agree with), use the Redirectors in this book—but in reverse. Turn the chit-chat *back* to more neutral territory like art, television, or the weather.

The so-called science of poll-taking is not a science at all but a mere necromancy. People are unpredictable by nature, and although you can take a nation's pulse, you can't be sure that the nation hasn't just run up a flight of stairs. —E. B. WHITE

grass•roots *adj* : characterizing a political movement that is spontaneous, local, and/or carried out by volunteers — "Let's start a **grassroots** movement to liberate the champagne from the refrigerator"

CUT FROM THE SAME CLOTH

Don't wear your political affiliations on your sleeve. Pins and buttons might win you points at a rally, but in mixed company they send a warning to those with opposing views. Then again, wearing the other team's colors can be used strategically (many politicians do this to suggest bipartisanship). While such a gesture might be lost on potential partners, presenting yourself without blatant bias is a sure way to increase your odds of engagement.

BOOZE IN THE BELTWAY

Toast your politics with a "Politician Cocktail." The drink, a strong mix of vodka, Irish cream, and milk, is finished off with a shot of Jägermeister. Consumers of the concoction say that it "starts off clean and ends dirty."

PICK A SIDE

The terms "left-wing" and "right-wing" were originally created during the French Revolution. Those who sat on the left side of the National Assembly favored revolutionary changes like the establishment of a republic; right-wingers typically supported keeping things the way they were. Generally speaking, the distinction is still true today. While both sides of the aisle (hopefully) have the best interest of their constituents in mind, those who identify as left-wing want to change the political status quo, while those who call themselves right-wing usually believe that things should be left well enough alone.

Speaking of the French, bring the conversation back to you with the all-purpose segue "speaking of . . . "

I have just received the following telegram from my generous Daddy. It says, "Dear Jack: Don't buy a single vote more than necessary. I'll be damned if I'm going to pay for a landslide. —JOHN F. KENNEDY

The tradition of the president throwing a ceremonial pitch began with William Howard Taft tossing the first ball of the league's opening day in 1910 at the soon-to-be-burned-to-the-ground National Park. While Bill Clinton was the first president to pitch successfully from the mound (others pitched from just in front of it), many agree that George W. Bush's opening pitch of the 2001 World Series—an almost perfect strike—was the best.

RHYMES OF THE TIMES

Although presidential hopefuls have flirted with the rhyming campaign slogan as far back as the mid-nineteenth century (e.g., William Henry Harrison's "Tippecanoe and Tyler Too"), candidates really embraced it during the 1940s. Following in the wake of the classic "I Like Ike" came a slew of poetic catchphrases, including "Madly for Adlai" (Adlai Stevenson), "All the Way with LBJ" (Lyndon B. Johnson), and "The Grin Will Win" (Jimmy Carter).

Turn this into a game to see who can come up with the best rhyme for a candidate—or even for someone in the room.

WE CAN, TOO

For both his 2004 senatorial campaign and his 2008 presidential run, Barack Obama repurposed the old union chant "Sí se puede" into the rallying cry of "Yes We Can." The phrase quickly became the centerpiece of Obama's political message. Meanwhile, several marketing-savvy companies decided that they, too, could catch a ride on the goodwill band-wagon. The most inspired? Ben & Jerry's "Yes Pecan!" ice cream.

IT'S ALL IN THE WRIST

The typical politician's handshake is firm, the perfect duration, and generally accompanied by a smile. Indeed, offering your hand to new acquaintances is a timeless means of engaging them. It's also a great way to make physical contact, decrease the distance between you and your partner, and create ideal chit-chat conditions. Be conscious, however, of standards among other cultures. A bow, while sacrificing physical contact, can impress in some circles.

Buzzkills have their sights set on making everyone as miserable as they are, so you'll have to counter their every uttering with your best political spin. Varnish the truth a little with some clever denial, bad news–burying, or simply cherry-picking facts that support a cheerier version of the buzzkill's story. Political corruption might be rampant, but it can also be juicy fun. A carefully placed euphemism will have everyone back in the partying spirit.

More men have been elected between Sundown and Sunup, than ever were elected between Sunup and Sundown.
—**WILL ROGERS**

COLOR THEORY

Prior to the 2000 election, using red and blue to signify political persuasion differed according to the media source. That election fixed the colors to their present-day meanings— red for Republicans and blue for Democrats.

HOME SWEET HOME

Founded as a federal district in 1790, the area that evolved into modern Washington DC was governed by Congress. Not until the passage of the District of Columbia Home Rule Act of 1973 were residents allowed to select their own officials. Nevertheless, despite being taxed in the same way as any other state, the district is granted no real vote in Congress. This has led to the wide adoption of the slogan, "Taxation without representation," a battle cry of the American Revolution. In its contemporary use, this phrase can be seen everywhere in DC, most noticeably on license plates. In a show of support, Bill Clinton even chose plates for the presidential limousine with the motto.

Taxes are hardly fare for light or upbeat banter. In fact, they can be downright depressing and off-putting—keep your distance.

Always be sincere,
even if you don't mean it.
—HARRY S. TRUMAN

It's not the voting that's democracy,
it's the counting. —TOM STOPPARD

....

SIXTH TIME WASN'T A CHARM

Norman Thomas ran six unsuccessful presidential campaigns in 1928, 1932, 1936, 1940, 1944, and 1948. Pat Paulsen, although mainly as a joke, ran eight times —in every election between 1968 and 1996.

BOOKS >

Sources claim that approximately sixteen thousand English-language books have been written about Abraham Lincoln, more than any other politician. Nobel Prize—winner President Jimmy Carter has made his own mark in the literary world, having penned nearly thirty books ranging from memoir to poetry to children's literature. It's usually agreed, however, that the greatest book ever written by a president is *The Personal Memoirs of Ulysses S. Grant*.

FOLLOW THE LEADER

Top players in the Beltway know everyone worth knowing. Likewise, in every social gathering, there's usually a top dog, the central nerve of the get-together, and your best resource for making introductions. Stay in close proximity to this person and, when appropriate, offer up a pertinent political tidbit to the group conversation. After interjecting, ask the host to introduce you to the rest of the guests. Before you know it, you could be the leader yourself.

truth•i•ness *n* : believing an idea's alleged veracity despite evidence to the contrary, coined by comedian Stephen Colbert — *see also* WMD — "I'm not too worried about the effects of eating cake—I've got **truthiness** on my side"

Vote for the man who promises least; he'll be the least disappointing. —BERNARD BARUCH

FOR FURTHER CONSIDERATION

Books

Rules of Civility and Decent Behaviour in Company and Conversation (ca. 1748), by George Washington

How to Win Friends and Influence People (1937), by Dale Carnegie

On the Road (1957), by Jack Kerouac

A People's History of the United States (1980), by Howard Zinn

On Speaking Well (1998), by Peggy Noonan

Film & Television

The Candidate (1972), directed by Michael Ritchie

The Daily Show with Jon Stewart (1996 premiere), created by Madeleine Smithberg and Lizz Winstead

Election (1999), directed by Alexander Payne

The Amazing Race (2001 premiere), created by Elise Doganieri and Bertram van Munster

Music

"The Star-Spangled Banner" (1814), by Francis Scott Key

"The Times They Are a-Changin'" (1964), sung by Bob Dylan

The First Term

BOLSTERING YOUR POSITION

Presidents are often judged by how much they accomplish in their first hundred days of office. Franklin D. Roosevelt, for example, was able to drive virtually the entire New Deal through Congress in his first three months, establishing the political high-water mark. While it's likely—and fortunate—that you'll never have to face that sort of pressure, you do have only a few precious minutes to make a favorable and sustainable impression on the group.

The more successful your introduction, the easier it will be to segue into meaningful chit-chat—and maintain that momentum. That's where this chapter comes in. Here, you'll encounter tips on remembering names and the importance of keeping an open mind throughout a conversation, all of which will help you keep the ball rolling.

You'll also learn to identify and interact with your audience, whether you're talking to a drunk (a familiar fixture at cocktail parties) or your boss (sometimes the same person!), and how to stick to topics that are light, not weighty or polarizing, until you can determine if you're dealing with an ally or an enemy. Furthermore, you'll have plenty of partisan stories and bureaucratic trivia in your arsenal to impress even the most senior member of Congress—or the party. Overall, you'll emerge from these pages with the know-how to make the rounds and garner your own brand of popular approval.

As any politician can tell you, however, even if you're well prepared and are off to a good start, it won't necessarily be smooth sailing from then on. Personalities often clash inexplicably, and the slightest flub can color a candidate's image. None of this should concern you, though; no matter how rocky your first few turns are, the most important thing is to stay positive.

In the grand arc of political careers, the first term is generally the most idealistic. Nonetheless, the reality of special interest groups, boring state dinners, and diminishing treasury resources (or, in conversational terms, the discovery of a know-it-all or disinterested partner) will soon settle in. For now, expect the best—you might just get it.

It's important for candidates to look directly into the camera during televised debates. Instead of focusing only on the moderator or the opposition, a candidate has the opportunity to make eye contact with millions of potential voters. At a gathering, you likely won't have to concentrate on more than one person at a time, but the lesson holds true. Making eye contact signals that you're invested in the conversation and have something important to contribute.

rogue *adj* : characterizing uncontrollable, unpredictable, defiant behavior — *see also* OUT OF LEFT FIELD, WTF — "The last time my hairdresser went **rogue**, I ended up with a mullet"

A COLD RECEPTION

The night of Grant's second inaugural ball, temperatures fell to 16 degrees. The weather turned the champagne into slush, caused violin strings to break, and resulted in the deaths of one hundred celebratory canaries.

> *If you want to rise in politics in the United States there is one subject you must stay away from, and that is politics.* —*GORE VIDAL*

....

SIT DOWN AND SHUT UP

Senator Strom Thurmond broke the record for the longest filibuster in history in 1957, with a speech of twenty-four hours and eighteen minutes, in protest of the Civil Rights Act. To prepare for the event, Thurmond visited the Senate steam room to reduce the amount of liquid in his body, ate an enormous sirloin steak, and sucked on lozenges and malted milk tablets. Among the items recited: the voting rights laws of every state; the Declaration of Independence; and the history of Anglo-Saxon juries. Thurmond's aide waited for him in the cloakroom with a pail in case the senator needed an emergency toilet. Fortunately, his antics were unsuccessful and the bill passed.

Steer clear of talking too much by being appropriately self-aware. Open your ears more often than your mouth.

I believe that truth is the glue that holds Government together, not only our Government, but civilization itself. —GERALD FORD

Reference this quote to counteract the vitriol of a particularly cynical conversationalist.

> HOLIDAYS

If it seems like your holiday season pushes the extremes of party attendance and cookie consumption, consider a December at the White House. In 2008, for example, the Bushes hosted 25 receptions, 7 holiday dinners, and mailed out 1.25 million cards. If that weren't enough, the traditional executive gingerbread house contained more than 475 pounds of gingerbread and white chocolate. And that's saying nothing about the executive manse itself. More than 780 feet of garland, 27 Christmas trees, 232 wreaths, and 412 poinsettias officially decked out the place. As for food, an estimated 22,000 Christmas cookies, 250 coconut cakes, 600 pounds of asparagus, and 700 gallons of eggnog were consumed. And to all a good night.

A MONUMENTAL FEAT

Despite common belief, there is no law that specifically states a Washington DC building cannot be taller than the Washington Monument. It is true, however, that the monument was for a short time the tallest building in the world. Completed in 1884 and standing at a triumphant 555 feet, 5 ⅛ inches tall, the monument wasn't unseated until 1889 with the completion of the Eiffel Tower, which came in at a dominating 1,063 feet.

THE DRUNK

Tread lightly when chatting up the drunk; heated debate is likely. Stick to safe subjects like presidential pets, something difficult to form a strong opinion on. If you find yourself drifting toward hot topics, lighten the mood by casually reminiscing about the booze-friendly presidency of Franklin D. Roosevelt, who famously said upon signing the twenty-first amendment ending Prohibition, "I believe this would be a good time for a beer."

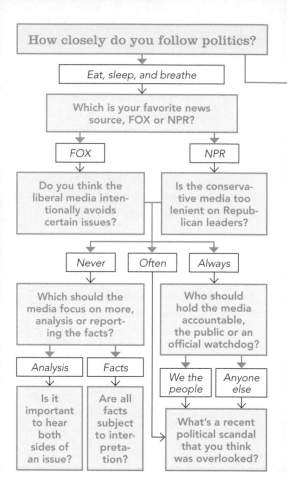

How closely do you follow politics?

Eat, sleep, and breathe

Which is your favorite news source, FOX or NPR?

FOX

Do you think the liberal media intentionally avoids certain issues?

NPR

Is the conservative media too lenient on Republican leaders?

Never | **Often** | **Always**

Which should the media focus on more, analysis or reporting the facts?

Who should hold the media accountable, the public or an official watchdog?

Analysis | **Facts**

Is it important to hear both sides of an issue?

Are all facts subject to interpretation?

We the people | **Anyone else**

What's a recent political scandal that you think was overlooked?

For some, following politics is a full-time job. For others, it ranks right below oral surgery. Knowing your partner's camp is vital to making a conversational game plan.

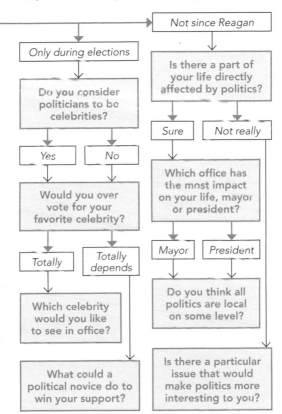

When it comes to food, the White House has historically been a fairly self-sustaining institution. Because presidents were required to support their own household, turning to the land around the executive residence has, until the mid-twentieth century, been a necessity. John Adams, for example, planted the first vegetable garden on the White House lawn. Andrew Jackson, smitten with citrus, created the "orangery," a greenhouse for growing tropical fruits that was later demolished to build the West Wing. The White House has also played host to a number of animals. Taft and his family got their milk from a pair of dairy cows, and the Wilson family raised sheep for wool and mutton.

Politics ... excites all that is selfish and ambitious in man.
—**DWIGHT D. EISENHOWER**

During the 2004 presidential race, an often-heard opinion cited George W. Bush as the candidate most voters would like to meet for a beer. By comparison, John Kerry was frequently portrayed as highbrow or, worse, aloof. As the election results proved, keeping your superiority complex in check can win people over. When conversing, avoid engaging in one-upmanship or flaunting your political smarts. And always make sure everyone's glass is full.

---

dou•ble•speak *n* : rhetoric that appears to communicate but does not — *syn* DOUBLETALK — *see also* GLITTERING GENERALITY, LOADED LANGUAGE, NEWSPEAK — "He used so much **doublespeak** that I was irritated twice"

. . . .

SIZE MATTERS

Compared to other speeches, such as MLK Jr.'s "I have a dream" speech (1,666 words) or JFK's inaugural address (1,364 words), Lincoln's Gettysburg Address contained 272 words, making it the most easily recited speech of all time.

IT'S JUST A NUMBER

The oldest elected president was Ronald Reagan at age 69; the youngest was John F. Kennedy at age 43. The youngest man to serve, however, was Theodore Roosevelt, at age 42, after succeeding the assassinated William McKinley. The oldest senator? The spry Strom Thurmond, who celebrated his 100th birthday in office. The youngest senator was the appointed John H. Eaton, from Tennessee. He was 28 upon entering office.

DECIDE TO BE UNDECIDED

Only days away from Election Day in the 2000 presidential race, it was reported that swing voters accounted for approximately 30 percent of all registered voters. Today, being on the fence is common. Use this position to your advantage the next time you're chatting up a person whose party affiliation is unclear. You'll learn which way they lean, and you'll also give them the pleasure of trying to sway your opinion. Who doesn't love a little debate?

It's a terribly hard job to spend a billion dollars and get your money's worth. —GEORGE M. HUMPHREY

....

READ UP!

In the White House, reading can take on a competitive edge. Between 2006 and 2008, the president and his deputy chief of staff Karl Rove reportedly held a contest to see who could read the most books in a single year. The outcome? Rove won all three years: 110 (Rove) to 95 (Bush) in 2006; 76 to 51 in 2007; and 64 to 40 in 2008. Perhaps the most impressive aspect of the competition, however, is the time required to read such a prodigious list.

"What are you reading?" is a great way to get to know someone and spark discussion.

Sitting tight is power.
—SAUL BELLOW

Given that about 34 percent of Americans claim to swing to the right, you can count on meeting a member of Lincoln's party just about anywhere you go. While they are often caricatured as reserved and bristly, it's folly to assume all Republicans are conservative on every issue. A fiscal conservative, for instance, could welcome the idea of gay marriage. Meanwhile, the most patriotic of Republican veterans might vehemently oppose war. As when engaging with any new acquaintance, proceed slowly, read body language, and try to explore a range of issues. Use the suggestions below as a guide, but always be prepared to improvise.

FOR:	AGAINST:
Tax cuts	New taxes
Big Oil	Big Government
Flags	Flag burning
Ann Coulter	Jon Stewart
Country music	Folk music
Texas	California
Global democracy	Illegal immigration
Executive legislation	Judicial legislation

RED, WHITE, BLUE, AND DELICIOUS

Fans of blueberry jellybeans can thank Ronald Reagan. The flavor was created for his inauguration, where he served red, white, and blue jellybeans—three and a half tons of them.

Always take the opportunity to ask new acquaintances about their likes and dislikes. Not everyone enjoys blue jellybeans, after all.

With words we govern men.
—BENJAMIN DISRAELI

THEATER

The Broadway musical *Camelot*, which opened in 1960, was based on the legend of King Arthur, and it epitomized the mythology of the Kennedy presidency. After JFK's assassination in 1963, Jacqueline Kennedy made a comparison between the Kennedy White House and the Tony Award–winning show, which was reportedly one of his favorites, by predicting "There'll be great presidents again . . . but there'll never be another Camelot."

> *[T]he cocktail party remains a vital*
> *Washington institution, the official intel-*
> *ligence system.* —BARBARA HOWAR

....

WAGE WARS

Do big decisions equal big bucks? Compare political salaries through the years (actual and adjusted
for inflation).

	PRESIDENT	**SENATOR**
• **1815:**	$25,000 *(361,000)*	$1,500 *(22,000)*
• **1873:**	$50,000 *(928,000)*	$5,000 *(92,800)*
• **1909:**	$75,000 *(1,830,800)*	$7,500 *(183,100)*
• **1949:**	$100,000 *(902,700)*	$12,500 *(112,800)*
• **1969:**	$200,000 *(1,174,300)*	$42,500 *(249,500)*
• **2001:**	$400,000 *(486,300)*	$145,100 *(176,400)*
• **2009:**	$400,000	$174,000

....

A ROSY AFFAIR

Each first lady is allowed to select one rose
variety that will bear her name. Private citizens
can also indulge in the rosy honor of having
a unique hybrid named for them. The cost
ranges from $7,500 to $30,000.

Score conversational points by remembering someone's name. Whether you've just been introduced or haven't chatted in years, this detail is vital to establishing a personal connection. Faced with addressing countless supporters, reporters, and donors every day, politicians have developed some handy tricks for remembering names, whether it's creating playful monikers or simply repeating the name several times. Careerbuilder.com suggests other helpful strategies, such as:

- Picture it written on the person's forehead
- Imagine writing it down
- Use word associations
- Use it frequently

Political language ... is designed to make lies sound truthful and murder respectable, and to give an appearance of solidity to pure wind. —**GEORGE ORWELL**

THE ENVIRONMENT

From lifting the ban on offshore drilling to rejecting limits on global warming, the Bush Administration's record on environmentalism probably isn't the shiniest jewel in its crown. Nevertheless, it did save roughly 20 tons of paper—about 480 trees—in 2008 by releasing the government's first paperless budget. In its printed form, the weighty tome would have filled four volumes, or about 2,200 pages of scintillating facts and figures.

WORTH A THOUSAND WORDS

Thomas Nast, the nineteenth-century editorial cartoonist who created our modern versions of the Democratic donkey, the Republican elephant, and Santa Claus, influenced American public opinion to such an extent that his cartoons could make or break a politician. Knowing it was wise to have him on their side, those aspiring to office curried favor with the cartoonist, even going so far as to bribe him to be cast in a favorable light.

When introducing new people to the group, give information about them that casts them in an engaging, positive light.

log•roll•ing *n* : the process of trading votes to effect an outcome that is favorable to both parties' interests — *syn* BACK-SCRATCHING, QUID PRO QUO — *see also* MUTUALLY ASSURED DESTRUCTION — "A sturdy marriage is only as solid as a couple's **logrolling** abilities"

I do not like broccoli. And I haven't liked it since I was a little kid and my mother made me eat it. And I'm president of the United States, and I'm not going to eat any more broccoli! —GEORGE H. W. BUSH

PLAY IT AGAIN, SAM

The fictional character of Uncle Sam was reportedly based on a real-life meatpacker from Troy, New York, named Samuel Wilson. The butcher provided the armed forces with beef and pork during the War of 1812, packaged in barrels branded with a "U.S." on the side. Officials joked that the initials stood for "Uncle Sam," a patrician character that soon came to represent the government itself.

Too bad that all the people who know how to run the country are busy driving taxicabs and cutting hair. —GEORGE BURNS

PICKY, PICKY

Over eleven thousand constitutional amendments have been put forth, but only twenty-seven have been ratified. The first grants free speech, free press, and the right to assemble. The most recent protects congressional salary.

POSITIVELY POLITICAL

While mudslinging might seem like the favorite pastime of campaigning politicians, the inevitable result is the painting of both candidates as unpleasant people. As your goal is to invite conversation, always be conscious of the attitude you're projecting. No matter what the topic is, pick something about the other person you can compliment. Once a warm, congenial tone is struck, your conversation should take a hospitable course.

During the workweek, the boss can be a source of frustration and discipline—but probably not much chit-chat. Striking up a conversation with a manager in a social setting doesn't have to be unpleasant, however. To make a good impression, be yourself, and recognize your partner's importance. Follow the example of Barack Obama, who displayed utmost respect for Bruce Springsteen when stating, "I'm the president, but he's the Boss."

OLD ENOUGH

Kyle Corbin, an eighteen-year-old college student, was elected mayor of Union, Oregon, after a write-in campaign in 2006. On Election Day, Corbin resided with his parents and was dating the captain of the cheerleading squad.

> *Idealism is the noble toga that political gentlemen drape over their will to power.* —*ALDOUS HUXLEY*

TELEVISION

They say that television adds ten pounds, but did you know it could also cost you an election? The first televised presidential debate occurred on September 26, 1960, between Senator John Kennedy and Vice President Richard Nixon, and it had a significant impact on American voters. While most viewers agreed that the candidates were equally matched on the issues, Nixon's unsightly five o'clock shadow and sickly pallor proved to be a big turnoff.

SHE RULES

Although women still have a ways to go for political parity, in 2007, Nancy Pelosi became the highest-ranking female politician in United States history, second in the line of succession and the first female Speaker of the House.

Get your facts first, and then you can distort them as much as you please. —MARK TWAIN

FOR FURTHER CONSIDERATION

Books

Where the Wild Things Are (1963),
by Maurice Sendak

Real Life at the White House (2002),
by John Whitcomb

On Bullshit (2005),
by Harry G. Frankfurt

How to Spot a Liar (2005),
by Gregory Hartley

The American Presidency, 5th ed. (2007),
by Sidney M. Milkis and Michael Nelson

Safire's Political Dictionary, revised
ed. (2008), by William Safire

Film & Television

Mr. Smith Goes to Washington
(1939), directed by Frank Capra

Spin City (1996 premiere), created by
Gary David Goldberg, Bill Lawrence, et al.

The West Wing (1999 premiere), created
by Aaron Sorkin

Music

"Hail to the Chief" (ca. 1812),
by James Sanderson

"Celebration" (1980), sung
by Kool & The Gang

Four More Years
MAINTAINING THE STATUS QUO

In politics, there's only one thing
better than a successful campaign—a
successful reelection campaign. And if
you're not in the game to win, what's
the point? The same holds true for
making chit-chat. With a few triumphant conversations under your belt,
you can now confidently up the ante.

By this point you've effectively estab-
lished yourself as a deft chit-chatter.
Just like congressional incumbents,
who gain a sweet 95 percent chance
of reelection over time, you'll have no
trouble connecting with those whom
you've talked up previously. Meanwhile, through word of mouth and

casual introductions, your sphere of conversational influence should now take on a life of its own, increasing without your having to lift a finger, or even open your mouth (but that's no fun).

So what are you going to do with your newfound popularity? One pitfall to avoid is letting your guard down. Resting on one's laurels, a common error of reelected politicians, is a sure way to drop a few rungs on the conversational ladder. Like a second-term president, you have gained the public's trust. Now, don't disappoint.

This chapter will help you keep things interesting—and avoid lame-duck status—from positing hard-hitting questions such as "Would you face imprisonment for your ideals?" to employing famous evasive (and extremely useful) one-liners. You'll also find helpful tips on managing alcohol intake and how to implement a filibuster. Finally, to keep yourself in check, remember the celebrated—but humbling—words of Michel de Montaigne, "On the highest throne in the world, we still sit only on our bottom."

No matter your success, always keep your head in the game. Stay focused—review the first two chapters before diving into a new situation. Improvising should come naturally to you by now, but you might want to refresh your material. Nothing will tarnish your reputation quicker than repeating the same story verbatim on several occasions. If needed, supplement your knowledge by scanning the politics section of the local newspaper. With replenished goods, you should be able to accomplish even your most ambitious conversational goals and ascend the throne of chit-chat greatness.

BLAZE OF GLORY

During a 1978 White House visit, Willie Nelson reportedly enjoyed a joint on the roof. Asked about it later, Nelson said, "My short-term memory is so bad I don't remember that. I'll check with Jimmy, see if he remembers."

Smoking's one redeeming quality is that it encourages camaraderie. Joining smokers on the terrace can stimulate chit-chat.

> CHILDREN

Who doesn't love a teddy bear? The favorite cuddly companion is named for huggable Theodore "Teddy" Roosevelt. On a hunting trip in Mississippi in 1902, Roosevelt refused to kill a bear his friends had clubbed and tied to a tree, thinking it would be unsportsmanlike. To commemorate the incident, the stuffed toy was created and soon became a national phenomenon. Even Roosevelt himself embraced the bear as a mascot in his reelection campaign.

> *Diplomacy is to do and say*
> *The nastiest thing in the nicest way.*
> —ISAAC GOLDBERG

Getting roped into a conversation with the know-it-all can be tedious, but don't despair; it's easier than you think to stump this intellectual windbag. Many can recall the most recent six or seven chief executives, but can your target name them all? What does the twenty-fourth amendment state (it eliminated the poll tax)? Remember, there's no need for *you* to know the answers; you simply need to prove that no one knows everything.

NEWS TO YOU

A 2004 study found that viewers of Comedy Central's *The Daily Show with Jon Stewart* understood the facts of that year's election better than those who watched the national nightly news or read newspapers. And while many argue against the show as a reliable source for news, a 2008 survey reported that regular watchers of *The Daily Show* were generally more informed than regular viewers of either *PBS NewsHour* or *The O'Reilly Factor*.

CHEERS

On July 30, 2009, President Barack Obama proved how useful alcohol can be to grease conversational wheels by holding his now famous "beer summit." Together with Harvard Professor Henry Louis Gates Jr. and the police officer who wrongfully arrested Gates, Sergeant James Crowley, Obama shared a cold one in the Rose Garden. Following this booze-fueled advice is a great idea for most social gatherings; alcohol is a surefire way of lowering inhibitions and loosening tongues. Perhaps it goes without saying, though, that a little bit goes a long way. A few too many and you could find yourself putting people off, becoming embroiled in a heated argument, or, worse, saying something you'll regret the next day.

KETCHUPGATE

A 1981 FDA proposal tried to reclassify ketchup and pickle relish as vegetables for use in public schools. Popularly known as "Ketchupgate," it was criticized by both Democrats and Republicans and was never implemented.

HAIR APPARENT

In politics, the hair just might make the man. Only five presidents have sported full beards while in office: Abraham Lincoln, Ulysses S. Grant, Rutherford B. Hayes, James Garfield, and Benjamin Harrison, the last to have a beard while serving, from 1889 to 1893. That doesn't mean, however, that every subsequent president was clean-shaven. Chester A. Arthur, William Taft, Theodore Roosevelt, and Grover Cleveland all had mustaches, while Martin Van Buren was known for his imposing muttonchops. All serious presidential candidates since the mustachioed Thomas E. Dewey—who lost to both Franklin D. Roosevelt and Harry S. Truman in the 1940s—have been sans facial hair.

> *Politics, n. A strife of interests mas-*
> *querading as a contest of principles.*
> *The conduct of public affairs for pri-*
> *vate advantage.* **—AMBROSE BIERCE**

Agree or disagree? Reference this quote to gauge everyone's level of cynicism vis-à-vis politics.

ear•marks *n pl* : legislative spending for a specific project or organization — ***see also*** PORK BARREL, INTEREST GROUP, BRIDGE TO NOWHERE — "I hope the new municipal budget has **earmarks** set aside for my taco-truck initiative"

....

THE NICK OF TIME

Abraham Lincoln might have enjoyed hearing himself referred to as "Honest Abe" or "The Great Emancipator," but not all presidential nicknames have been as lofty. A few of the less memorable were:

- His Rotundity, John Adams
- His Little Majesty, James Madison
- His Accidency, John Tyler
- Ten-Cent Jimmie, James Buchanan
- Granny, Rutherford B. Hayes
- The Dude President, Chester A. Arthur
- The Elephantine Economist, Grover Cleveland
- The Human Iceberg, Benjamin Harrison
- The Phrasemaker, Woodrow Wilson
- Wobbly Warren, Warren G. Harding

Have fun with your fellow chit-chatters by devising secret nicknames for the other partygoers.

Men must turn square corners when they deal with the Government.
—OLIVER WENDELL HOLMES JR.

THE MEDIA

When breaking the big news, sometimes haste makes waste. Perhaps most famously, the *Chicago Tribune's* headline blunder of the 1948 presidential election erroneously claimed Thomas E. Dewey as the victor instead of Harry S. Truman. This wasn't the first time newspapers had published incorrect results, however. In the close presidential election of 1916, many New York papers called the race early for candidate Charles Evans Hughes. Yet the next morning, the tally revealed that Woodrow Wilson had narrowly taken California, winning him the race. More recently, the *New York Post* ran a headline announcing John Kerry's running mate as Dick Gephardt, much to John Edwards's chagrin.

Politics makes strange bedfellows.
—PROVERB

THE HOTTIE

Looks mean a lot in politics. A Stanford University study suggested that candidates can gain as much as 20 percent in polls by changing their appearance so they look more like their electorate. If you feel like you're out of your league when talking to a hottie, do your best to match their posture and vocal patterns. The emulation will appeal to his or her sense of vanity, promoting a stronger conversational, or more, connection.

POTTY MOUTH

In 1999, while debating legislation in the House that would require all new toilets to be low-flow, North Carolina Rep. Richard Burr caused a splash by transcribing his remarks onto a roll of toilet paper.

THE COMMISH

Former Secretary of State Condoleezza Rice
has revealed in numerous interviews that her
dream job is to be the Commissioner of the
National Football League. In fact, she's seen
every Super Bowl since its inception in 1967.

FILIBUSTER

Filibustering is a complex art that is nevertheless worth mastering; it can come in handy
when faced with an uncomfortable pause in conversation. Fill the lull by taking the lead. Use
the last topic as a starting point to pontificate,
elaborating as extensively as possible to occupy
as much airtime as possible (like this sentence).
Remember, dominating the conversation is
inherently rude, so your goal should be to buy
enough time only to set plan B in motion.

Under every stone lurks a politician.
—ARISTOPHANES

P.A.T.R.I.O.T.

The USA PATRIOT Act isn't just a clever name. This heavily contrived acronym stands for "Uniting and Strengthening America by Providing Appropriate Tools Required to Intercept and Obstruct Terrorism."

> HEALTH

Politicians today enjoy the perks of modern medicine and a government health care plan, but the founding fathers had a decidedly harder time taking care of themselves. Washington's infamously bad teeth caused him no small amount of discomfort. With only one original tooth in his mouth, he wore dentures made of various materials (from ivory to gold) and wire. Although the stress of political office still takes a toll on the body, contemporary politicians have been able to make light of their aches and pains. Former Vice President Dick Cheney, who has suffered five heart attacks (at the time this book was printed), once made light of his health problems, saying, "Except for the occasional heart attack, I never felt better."

....

EVASIVE ONE-LINERS

- "I am not a crook." —Richard Nixon
- "I haven't committed a crime. What I did was fail to comply with the law." —David Dinkins
- "I didn't accept it. I received it." —Richard Allen
- "It depends upon what the meaning of 'is' is." —Bill Clinton
- "I'm a fairly wide guy . . . I had to spread my legs." —Larry Craig

Although these gems probably won't work for you, have a few all-purpose lines at the ready to dodge conversational bullets.

> *On the highest throne in the world,*
> *we still sit only on our own bottom.*
> —*MICHEL DE MONTAIGNE*

....

BILL COSBY: PUBLIC ENEMY

Nixon kept an "Enemies List," a collection of his major political opponents, including Bill Cosby, Jane Fonda, Carol Channing, Barbra Streisand, John Lennon, Paul Newman, Joe Namath, Ted Kennedy, the *New York Times*, and the *Washington Post*.

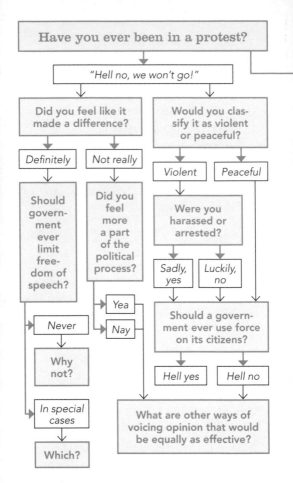

If a person has spent time on the picket line, expect an earful of strong opinions. If protests and your target don't mix, try asking questions that force one to pick a side.

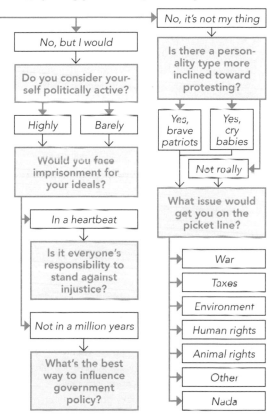

Members of Congress certainly don't shake on every compromise. Still, it's generally true that nothing says "détente" like a well-executed hand gesture. If a conversational misstep leaves your fellow chit-chatter glancing at the clock, reengage by opening your arms, turning your palms up submissively, and affirming that your partner seems much more informed on the issue. An unobtrusive pat on the shoulder can also be used to promote understanding.

> *Once a decision was made, I did not worry about it afterward.*
> —*HARRY S. TRUMAN*

....

PREDATORY POLITICOS

Jesse "The Body" Ventura, future governor of Minnesota, starred in the 1987 movie *Predator* with future California governor Arnold Schwarzenegger and Sonny Landham, who unsuccessfully ran for the Kentucky governorship.

lame duck *n* **1** : a politician nearing the end of his or her tenure **2** : a politician who has lost political power **3** : one who is ineffectual or lacks ability — *see also* ENFEEBLED, FAIL — "Mom, you're not a **lame duck**—I still listen to your advice"

Avoid lame-duck status by knowing when to make an exit, like when your audience starts to shift and fidget.

> *Modern politics is, at bottom, a struggle not of men but of forces.* —*HENRY ADAMS*

TRAVEL

Spending most of the time on the road is a fact of life for many politicians. While candidates today can expect to travel hundreds of thousands of miles crisscrossing the country, it's hard to top the estimated 350,000 miles in 399 railroad trips that Franklin D. Roosevelt covered during his presidency. Luckily for the public trust, campaign trips are paid for primarily by the candidates themselves (an exemption is made for Secret Service personnel).

*I believe there is something out there
watching over us. Unfortunately, it's
the government.* —**WOODY ALLEN**

*This is a great quote to pull out if there's a Libertarian among you.
Then, sit back and enjoy the verbal fireworks.*

THE GREEN PARTY MEMBER

Looking for a conversation starter with a member of the Green Party? Try: "What, really, is the difference between the Republicans and the Democrats?" The punch line, of course, is "nothing." The Green Party has been seeking an answer to the two-party system since the mid-1980s, officially becoming the "Green Party of the United States" in 2001. You should probably try not to mention the common theory that Ralph Nader made a critical difference during the 2000 presidential election, taking likely left-leaning votes away from Democrat Al Gore. Instead, stick to the party's defining issue— the environment and, more specifically, how to protect it. What you learn just might leave you questioning your own party choice.

Stating that then–presidential hopeful Barack Obama "has more clichés in his vocabulary than you can shake a stick at," Irish bookmaking agency Paddy Power actually took bets on which phrases Obama would use when accepting the Democratic nomination in 2008. He failed to utter it, but "I'm fired up" was the favorite with six-to-one odds. Some pundits have speculated that American politicians are almost obliged to speak in clichés to avoid scaring off potential voters; generalities communicated in the form of dependable, albeit bland, clichés are apparently more easily digested by the unwashed masses. At any rate, given popular appraisal of Obama as a masterful orator, it seems that having a ready arsenal of platitudes is never a bad idea. While they might not add much in the way of content, clichés do help move a stalled conversation forward by acting as ready filler for awkward pauses. You can't argue with odd nuggets of wisdom such as, "Know thyself." Who knows? You could even score points by dropping a polished, if oft-used, turn of phrase. After all, it is what it is.

ART

Politics and art can occasionally make for a fishy mix. In 2005, Alaska Airlines was given a federal grant of $500,000 to promote Alaskan seafood. The money was used to paint the length of a Boeing 737 with the image of a salmon. Known to many as the "Salmon-Thirty-Salmon," the job took a team of thirty painters twenty-four days to finish. Mark Boyle, the artist, said that the biggest challenge was "to make it anatomically correct."

Few men have virtue to withstand the highest bidder.
—GEORGE WASHINGTON

V-I-C-T-O-R-Y!

Getting people excited is essential to being a good politician, so it makes sense that pols such as George W. Bush, Ronald Reagan, Dwight D. Eisenhower, and Franklin D. Roosevelt were all former cheerleaders.

....

THE POLITICAL LIFE

The trajectory of the politician's career—indeed, life itself—follows a familiar path. Typical political milestones (by age):

- **10:** Debates with parents; wins, again
- **19:** Matriculates into Harvard
- **21–25:** Earns six figure income at family firm
- **26:** Mounts first campaign, focuses on local issues, loses
- **27:** Mounts second campaign, focuses on outspending opponent, wins
- **30:** Taps shady business associates to finance national campaign
- **30–50:** Wins broad base of support; secures position in Congress
- **51:** Runs for president
- **52–56:** First term, generally avoids scandal
- **56–60:** Second term, secures legacy and/or suffers impeachment
- **61+:** Writes memoirs, has library named in honor

Giving money and power to government is like giving whisky and car keys to teenage boys. —P. J. O'ROURKE

Imagine how entertaining debates in the Senate would be with only five senators (read: not very). In conversation, as in the Senate, the more the merrier. If your tête-à-tête is beginning to lose steam, find an unsuspecting third party nearby and engage the newcomer with an appropriate, direct question such as, "Don't you agree, John?" This trick can be used several times in a row to build a small, focused group. Soon, lively banter will abound.

pun•dit *n* : one with many opinions who comments or judges authoritatively, usu. through a form of mass media — *syn* TALKING HEAD, CRITIC, COMMENTATOR — "He's got great hair for a **pundit**"

Being in politics is like being a football coach. You have to be smart enough to understand the game, and dumb enough to think it's important. —EUGENE MCCARTHY

FOR FURTHER CONSIDERATION

Books

Democracy in America (1835),
by Alexis de Tocqueville

The Communist Manifesto (1848),
by Karl Marx and Friedrich Engels

The Power Broker (1974), by Robert A. Caro

Groupthink (1982), by Irving L. Janis

The Partly Cloudy Patriot (2002),
by Sarah Vowell

Film & Television

Dangerous Liaisons (1988),
directed by Stephen Frears

Groundhog Day (1993), directed
by Harold Ramis

True Lies (1994), directed
by James Cameron

Wag the Dog (1997), directed
by Barry Levinson

Deal or No Deal (2005 premiere),
created by Dick de Rijk

Music

"Respect" (1965),
sung by Aretha Franklin

"One More Time" (2002),
sung by Daft Punk

Impeachment

BOWING OUT GRACEFULLY

Every great political career must come to an end, and the same goes for conversations. But while politicians don't always have the luxury of foretelling the circumstances of their departure, whether they leave mired in a salacious sex scandal or simply step down after their tenure is up, savvy conversationalists should be able to dictate how and when their own exit occurs.

In this chapter, you'll acquire the knowledge necessary to choose how you bow out. For your parting lines, you might recite an innocuous fact or drop a shocking anecdote, or you might toss out a memorable quote or introduce someone as a conversational replacement. You'll also learn what to do if you encounter someone else with this book—whether you engage or evade them—and how to recover if you inadvertently "pull a Joe Biden," i.e., make a gaffe.

Conversations can take a bad turn, but do your best to keep your composure. Change topics or, if unsalvageable, abandon ship altogether. If you're the one responsible for the souring, try not to dwell on the slipup any longer than you have to—and especially avoid repeating your denial overzealously. Learn from the mistakes of disgraced former-President Richard Nixon, whose many vocal appeals to his innocence during the Watergate scandal made him look like *more* of a crook, if anything.

Of course, not all conversations are destined to end as terribly as the Nixon Administration, and perhaps the truest test of a professional chit-chatter is knowing when a conversation has simply run its course (like the Clinton Administration). Though it's impossible to plan for every contingency, you can certainly tip the scales in your favor by always having a few exit strategies up your sleeve. Whichever departure route you choose, be sure that you're also leaving a good impression behind—especially while you're ahead. You might think the race is over, but who knows, your illustrious chit-chat career could be just beginning.

A little rebellion now and then is a good thing.
—*THOMAS JEFFERSON*

....

IF YOU DON'T SECEDE

Since the Republic of Texas was annexed by the United States in 1845, the idea of secession has had a place at the table. Although an official defection did briefly occur during the Civil War (Texas was readmitted as a state in 1870), the modern movement to secede was mostly quiet until 2009 when Texas Governor Rick Perry hinted that the Lone Star State had always reserved the right to leave the Union, since the state wasn't technically acquired legally. Public opinion polls in Texas taken after the governor's comments offered more food for thought. In one, 40 percent of those polled and 48 percent of Texas Republicans were in favor of secession.

....

MINT CONDITION

Printed in 1934 with the portrait of Woodrow Wilson, the $100,000 bill is the largest denomination of paper money in the United States. But what about the bill's smaller, less elusive (yet rare) cousin, the $2 bill? Despite popular belief to the contrary, it's still in circulation (as of 2007, the treasury reported over $1.5 billion worth of the bills in the marketplace), although additional printings are seldom requested.

If you happen to have a $100,000 bill in your pocket (or in your bank account), keep it there; no one likes a braggart.

PUT IT TO A VOTE

With its earliest origins in ancient Greece and ancient Rome, voting—the cornerstone of democracy—is a tried and-true method of defusing an exchange turned volatile. If you and your partner have reached an impasse, suggest putting it to a vote. A formal process is unnecessary, of course; simply ask those around you to say "yea" or "nay." Chances are at least one person will share your opinion, which will take the focus partially off you.

A study by the National Opinion Research Center revealed that extreme liberals have the most sex, extreme conservatives have slightly less, and moderates have the least. Not all encounters, however, involve husbands and wives. *Newsweek* compiled a list of the major political sex scandals since 1976 and found that dalliances were almost equally distributed between Democrats and Republicans—but only one involved a female politician.

-gate *n suffix* : an appendage term used to imply a scandal, usu. creating outrage or disgrace, <LIPSTICKGATE>, <KETCHUPGATE> — ***see also*** MEDIA SPIN — "We're just out of gin—stop saying 'martini**gate**'"

TUNNEL OF LOVE

The "Marilyn entrance," named for the movie star with whom JFK purportedly had an affair, is the opening to an alleged tunnel running under the East Wing to the Treasury Building. It's believed Monroe never set foot in it.

> *Hell hath no fury like a*
> *bureaucrat scorned.*
> —*MILTON FRIEDMAN*

THE BORE

Left unchecked, the bore will happily spend hours filling your ear with a steady monotone of inane political facts. The goal is to extricate yourself without investing too much time or energy, as well as not hurting anyone's feelings. Your best course of action is to pass the buck. Just as JFK's grandfather, "Honey Fitz" Fitzgerald, did with the fabled "Irish Switch"— shaking a voter's hand while talking to a second voter and winking at a third—establish eye contact with someone else, wave them over, catch them up on the topic of conversation, and then politely make your escape. You could either stop there or, if the pain in your replacement's eyes is too much to bear, send someone else in a few minutes for relief.

💡 MAKE A U-TURN

Flip-flopping politicians are common, but history has shown that a few well-executed flips do not necessarily lead to a political flop. The same goes for conversation. If you've made an offensive remark, immediately laugh and play it off as a joke. Or, if you've missed that window of opportunity, feign ignorance on the issue, let your partner explain their position, apologize sincerely, and then switch subjects as quickly as possible.

Corruption is nature's way of restoring our faith in democracy. —**PETER USTINOV**

IN THE KNOW

Amid the Clinton sex scandal, comedian and future Minnesota Senator Al Franken and friend John Markus published a full-page appeal in the *New York Times* to Kenneth Starr, pleading, "Dear Ken: Please subpoena us. We know things."

He knows nothing; and he thinks he knows everything. That points clearly to a political career.
—GEORGE BERNARD SHAW

. . . .

MADCAP MISHAPS

Every so often, a politico is caught up in an incident so absurd that it keeps late-night talk show hosts in jokes for weeks. Some of the more amazing episodes include Bush Sr.'s vomiting into the lap of former Japanese Prime Minister Kiichi Miyazawa after losing a grueling tennis match with the Emperor of Japan; Bush Jr.'s "shoe attack," when Iraqi journalist Muntadar al-Zaidi threw his shoes during a press conference, calling the president a "dog"; Dick Cheney's hunting disaster, when he shot the face of a seventy-eight-year-old friend while hunting quail in Texas; and Jimmy Carter's "killer rabbit" attack, when a swamp rabbit gone berserk tried to take down the vacationing chief exec in a fishing boat.

Deal with insane swamp rabbits and heated chit-chat similarly. Project calmness and reassurance by lowering your voice.

quis•ling *n* : a traitor or collaborator, attributed to Vidkun Quisling, a Norwegian politician and Nazi sympathizer — *syn* DOUBLE-CROSSER, TURNCOAT — "Everyone knows you voted for Nader, you **quisling**"

....

2008: ANOTHER SCANDALOUS YEAR

In a snapshot of a single inglorious year, these are the liaisons that made the news:

- **January:** Kwame Kilpatrick (D), sexting
- **March:** Eliot Spitzer (D), prostitution scandal
- **March:** David Paterson (D), admitted to extramarital affairs
- **May:** Marc Dann (D), affair with a staffer
- **May:** Vito Fossella (R), affair with a retired air force colonel
- **August:** John Edwards (D), affair with a campaign employee
- **October:** Tim Mahoney (D), multiple affairs

As so often happens with Washington scandals, it isn't the original scandal that gets people in the most trouble—it's the attempted cover-up. —TOM PETRI

> *Finality is not the language of politics.*
> —*BENJAMIN DISRAELI*

....

CRIB NOTES

In early 2010, Sarah Palin addressed a crowd
with notes scrawled on the palm of her hand.
Among the prompts: "Lift American Spirits."
If she had used this book, she could have
avoided all the fuss.

*To ensure you're seen as a natural conversationalist, avoid this
Palin method of chit-chat. Be spontaneous.*

VACATION

Thanks to Eisenhower's Interstate Highway System, roadtrips are an enjoyable—and
economical—way to take a family vacation.
Thinking of more than just holidays, though,
Ike's primary goal was to provide citizens with
an escape route from cities if the nation came
under attack from Cold War adversaries. Every
year, more than one trillion miles are traveled
on the Interstate Highway System—some of
them more pleasurable than others.

LOST IN TRANSLATION

The urban legend states that, on a trip to West Berlin in 1963, JFK, trying to say in German, "I'm a Berliner," actually uttered, "I'm a jelly donut." Linguists still argue over which is correct. Purists contend that Kennedy's declaration mentions fried dough explicitly, while others feel that this interpretation is too literal. However you look at it, the "Jelly Donut" speech has taken on a life of its own.

THE EX

There's no shame in running into your ex. Regardless of who ended it, both of you can find a silver lining in the most closely held American ideal—freedom. Let it ring by touching on those political topics that were taboo while you were together. Although talking politics is usually a surefire way to spark confrontation, in this scenario, it'll let you get some things off your chest *and* help you avoid the truly touchy subject— who you're dating now.

For every political fiasco, there's always a fall guy. Richard G. Darman, George H. W. Bush's budget director, explained away the commander in chief's broken campaign promise about wetland preservation by stating, "He didn't say that. He read what was given to him in a speech." Although it would be nice to have a personal speechwriter, blaming one for your verbal blunders probably isn't your best bet. Nevertheless, it's easy to pass the buck when you find yourself guilty of a conversational misstep. If someone is obviously put off by one of your quips or facts, claim that an unreliable coworker gave you the information, and allow the person to discredit the item. Or, you could always blame this book.

You can fool too many of the people too much of the time.
—*JAMES THURBER*

While movie acting is one way to get into politics—Ronald Reagan, Arnold Schwarzenegger, and Clint Eastwood all come to mind—politicians with minimal stage experience tend to limit their cameos to the smaller screen: Richard Nixon appeared on *Rowan & Martin's Laugh-In* (with the famous line, "Sock it to me!"); Gerald Ford was a guest on *Dynasty*; Jimmy Carter on *Home Improvement*; and Al Gore on *30 Rock* (all played themselves).

FREEDOM FRIES

In 2003, France opposed the American position on Iraq, and Republican lawmakers were offended. North Carolina Rep. Walter B. Jones and Ohio Rep. Bob Ney, in response to what Jones called France's "self-serving politics of passive aggression," took matters into their own hands and officially changed the menu of the House cafeterias to read "Freedom fries." The French Embassy pointed out that French fries actually come from Belgium.

Everyone loves greasy food, but be careful; one slip and your nibbles will become dribbles, which could be embarrassing.

Human blunders, however,
usually do more to shape history
than human wickedness.
—A. J. P. TAYLOR

SEX, DRUGS, AND SCANDAL

Used in moderation, gossip can be an invaluable way to stoke the flames of discussion. After all, there's no denying that the illicit sexual predilections of a philandering politician are more captivating than routine changes to zoning laws. But engaging in gossip can also be dangerous if taken too far. Blithely chewing the fat about wayward celebrities or politicians is one thing (provided they're not present, of course); just be cautious of the conversation turning toward personal contacts or others in the room. If it does, do an about-face, and say the first thing that comes to mind (e.g., "Bananas!"). A non sequitur will probably make for an awkward segue, but it'll also instantly put the conversation back on a safe path.

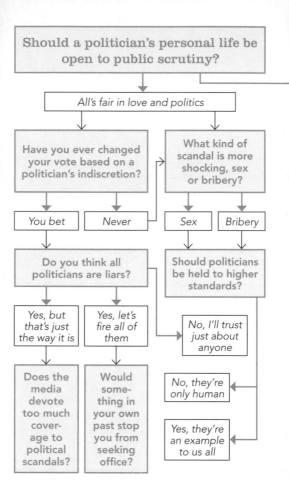

Should a politician's personal life be open to public scrutiny?

All's fair in love and politics

Have you ever changed your vote based on a politician's indiscretion?

What kind of scandal is more shocking, sex or bribery?

You bet *Never* *Sex* *Bribery*

Do you think all politicians are liars?

Should politicians be held to higher standards?

Yes, but that's just the way it is *Yes, let's fire all of them*

No, I'll trust just about anyone

Does the media devote too much coverage to political scandals?

Would something in your own past stop you from seeking office?

No, they're only human

Yes, they're an example to us all

Politicians have a seemingly endless supply of dirty laundry to air. Find out how nosy your partner is by asking the right question: is it a private life, or is it public record?

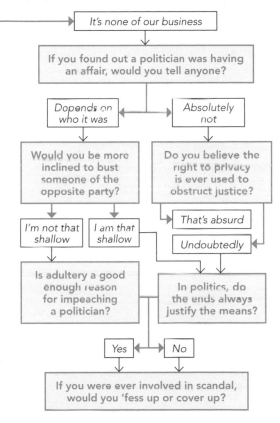

It's none of our business

If you found out a politician was having an affair, would you tell anyone?

Depends on who it was — Absolutely not

Would you be more inclined to bust someone of the opposite party?

Do you believe the right to privacy is ever used to obstruct justice?

I'm not that shallow — I am that shallow

That's absurd

Undoubtedly

Is adultery a good enough reason for impeaching a politician?

In politics, do the ends always justify the means?

Yes — No

If you were ever involved in scandal, would you 'fess up or cover up?

YOUR FELLOW CHIT-CHATTER

You may notice, in the course of a conversation, someone who is as clever, witty, and charming as you—a master orator of the highest order. This person can make a fascinating entrance, effortlessly join a group, engage others in delightful conversation, and exit the scene gracefully. Bons mots and factoids emerge from their lips, and others at the event are held in thrall to this enchanting raconteur. That person, without a doubt, owns a copy of this book. Subtly make contact so that the two of you can steer clear of complications, and execute a secret sign (known only to those who have read this book): the old con man's tell—placing a finger to the side of the nose. Conversational catastrophe averted.

CLOAK AND DAGGER

To make contact, Bob Woodward's Watergate informant "Deep Throat" drew a clock on the reporter's newspaper indicating the time they'd meet. Woodward responded by moving the flowerpot on his front porch.

> *Power is the great aphrodisiac.*
> *—HENRY KISSINGER*

. . . .

BELIEVE IT OR NOT

The only openly atheist member of the United States Congress is Pete Stark, a Democrat from Fremont, California. Although he identifies as a Unitarian, he declared publicly he doesn't believe in a "supreme being."

It's best to avoid religion when chit-chatting, but if it comes up, try to keep the conversation general and non-confrontational.

MONEY

Who says politics doesn't pay? Senators and members of the House receive an annual salary of $174,000. The minority and majority party leaders each earn $193,400. The president takes home a $400,000 annual salary, along with other perks, including $19,000 for entertainment. One of the lowest paid politicians, however, is Mayor Michael Bloomberg of New York. Worth an estimated $16 billion, the mayor elected to receive a salary of only $1 per year.

bul•ly pul•pit *n* : a platform, usu. high-ranking, from which to influence opinion — ***see also*** POLITICAL AGENDA — "Unlike everyone else, I fully admit that my blog is a **bully pulpit**"

Politics is supposed to be the second oldest profession. I have come to realize that it bears a very close resemblance to the first.
—RONALD REAGAN

....

THE FORGIVING CITY

Whoever thinks there are no second chances in politics has only to look to the local government of our nation's capital. In 1992, after three-term mayor Marion Barry was charged with three counts of felony perjury, ten counts of misdemeanor drug possession, and one count of misdemeanor conspiracy to possess cocaine, he was still reelected to the DC city council. Two years later, Barry was once again elected as the city's mayor.

Everyone deserves a second chance. Don't write someone off immediately if their conversation skills aren't as honed as yours.

. . . .

THIS JUST IN . . .

The non-scandal scandal has always been a great source of DC reportage. In 2007, then-Senator Hillary Clinton displayed more cleavage than usual, and media outlets went wild. "Boobgate" was born (and quickly died).

It goes without saying that you should steer clear of sexist banter—especially with a new friend.

LAME DUCK

Some conversations just won't get off the ground. In these cases, go out in a blaze of glory. Instead of pandering to your fellow conversationalists, say what's on your mind, whether it's that the Supreme Court stinks, politics are a joke, or you'd rather live in China. Brace yourself; this approach could end the conversation abruptly. Then again, they might find your candor refreshing. Either way, this last-ditch tactic is certain to shake things up.

> *Nothing is so admirable in*
> *politics as a short memory.*
> —*JOHN KENNETH GALBRAITH*

While most politicians are eager to support policies aimed at reducing global warming, a 2007 amendment forced policymakers to switch to more fuel-efficient cars for official business, such as the Toyota Prius (a car, many noted, not made in the United States). Setting an example for his colleagues, the amendment's primary proponent, Emanuel Cleaver II (D-MO), has settled on a recycled airport shuttle fueled by cooking grease to be used as his mobile office.

NO CLASS

In the 1960 election, when victory was finally called for John F. Kennedy, Richard Nixon decided not to deliver an official concession speech. Instead, he sent a telegram, which a staffer read aloud later on television. Kennedy's response? "No class."

Nobody believes a rumor here in Washington until it's officially denied.
—EDWARD CHEYFITZ

FOR FURTHER CONSIDERATION

Books

The End of the Affair (1951),
by Graham Greene

Where the Sidewalk Ends (1974),
by Shel Silverstein

All the President's Men (1974),
by Bob Woodward

How to Write Your Own Life Story
(1997), by Lois Daniel

*The Executive's Guide to Finding a
New Job* (2009), by Nicholas Pierce

Film & Television

Advise & Consent (1962), directed
by Otto Preminger

Happy Days (1974 premiere), created
by Garry Marshall

Sex, Lies, and Videotape (1989),
directed by Steven Soderbergh

Music

"The End" (1967), sung by The Doors

"Bridge over Troubled Water" (1970),
sung by Simon & Garfunkel

"Another One Bites the Dust"
(1980), sung by Queen

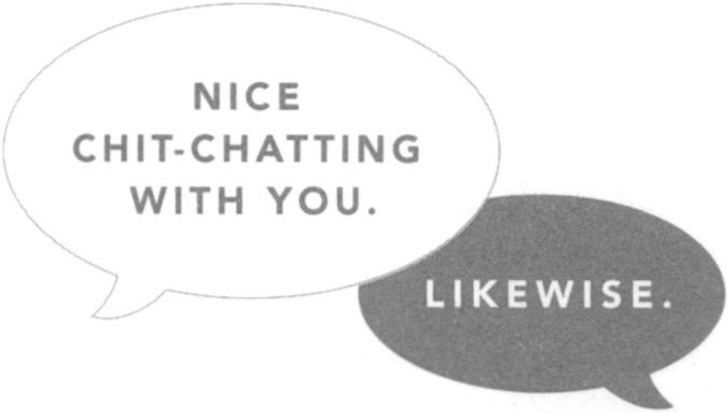
NICE CHIT-CHATTING WITH YOU.
LIKEWISE.